Giotto

in the
Chapel of the Scrovegni

MEDOACVS

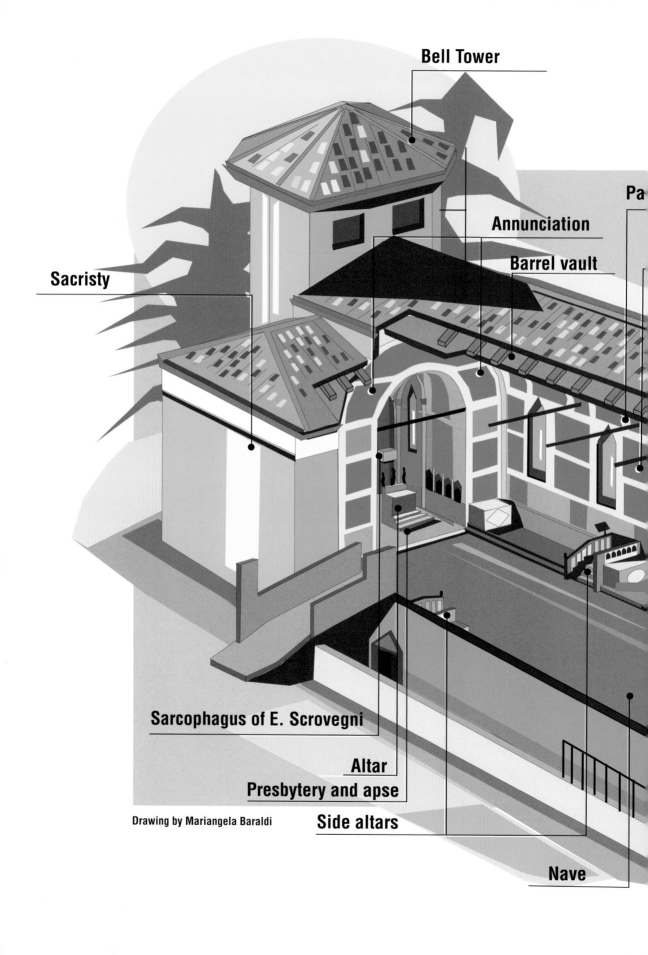

Bell Tower

Annunciation

Barrel vault

Pa

Sacristy

Sarcophagus of E. Scrovegni

Altar

Presbytery and apse

Side altars

Drawing by Mariangela Baraldi

Nave

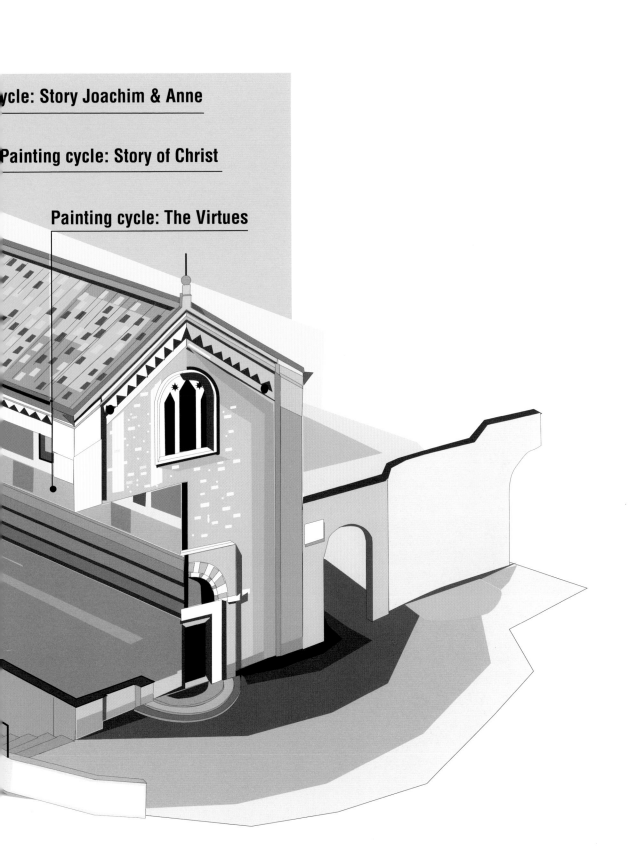

ycle: Story Joachim & Anne

Painting cycle: Story of Christ

Painting cycle: The Virtues

GIOTTO DI BONDONE

Painter and architect, the most representative artist of the Middle Ages was born at Colle di Vespignano, near Vicchio in the Mugello, about the year 1267. Giotto enjoyed a great reputation in his own day and the famous acknowledgement contained in Dante's verses in the *Purgatory,* canto XI, vv. 94-96:

Cimabue thought to hold the field in painting,
 and now Giotto hath the cry,
 so that the fame of the other is obscured.

Although well-documented, the sources dealing with Giotto's debut are rather vague on details, so it is not possible to trace an historical outline based on certainty. Even though his activity in the Basilica of San Francesco at Assisi was noted in 1313 by Riccobaldo da Ferrara and, in the following centuries, by notables such as Ghiberti and Vasari, the question as to the real extent of his involvement remains open. The problem is complicated by the fact that there are two churches, and that Giotto worked on both. Most present-day critics, however, would agree in attributing to him the frescoes on *The Life of St Francis* - in the nave of the upper church of San Francesco of Assisi - mainly basing this assumption on stylistic analysis. The decorations in the basilica do contain, in point of fact, "such a concentration of figurative innovations as to be inevitably considered the crucial point in the change that took place in Italian painting between the last decades of the thirteenth century and the beginning of the fourteenth". In the last decade of the 13thC Giotto went to Rome several times, enlarging his direct knowledge of classical painting and of the works of Cavallini and of Arnolfo di Cambio. Alas, there is but fragmentary evidence of that sojourn in the Eternal City that was so vital for the evolution of the classical elements of his art. There is the *Cross* of Aracoeli, the tondi of the prophets in the left transept of the Basilica of Santa Maria Maggiore, and the fresco depicting Bonifacio VIII between two clerics in the Basilica of St John Lateran. To these same years belong the *Crucifixion* in the Malatesta Temple at Rimini, damaged on the outer tips of the arms of the cross but stylistically very similar to the Crucifix he executed for the Chapel of the Scrovegni. When Giotto reached Padua he was the most renowned painter in Italy. Perhaps he had been invited there by the friars of the Basilica of the Saint to paint the frescoes in their Chapterhouse; whatever the case, he worked in Padua over a long period of time and returned several times at the request of his patrons. Of all this activity, only the cycle of frescoes in the Chapel of the Scrovegni remains, since those in the Basilica of St Anthony were lost, and likewise those in the Hall of Justice, the *Palazzo della Ragione*. Giotto's arrival signalled a revolutionary change in pictorial language, carried to such an extent that its effects on Veneto culture were to be felt right into the second half of the 14thC. It is Giotto who affirms the three-dimensionality of space into which his figures and events are placed realistically, seeming to have a life of their own. The observer experiences a feeling of "presence" - the sensation that

something has taken place; and, when there has been time to reflect more carefully and profoundly on the scenes, becomes aware of the profoundly significant symbolism underlying the purposeful plan of the cycle. The Paduans were quick to appreciate Giotto's originality and some years later engaged him to decorate the building that stood out as the symbol and pride of their citizenship, the Hall of Justice. Between 1307 and 1308 Giotto was back in Assisi working on the frescoes in the Magdalen Chapel in the lower basilica. Around the year 1311 he made a second journey to Rome to execute the mosaic of the Fishing Boat, which is now in the portico of the Basilica of St Peter, opposite the entrance doors: of the original mosaic work, only two fragments remain - busts of angels, which however have been reset many times. There is considerable controversy too over the dating of the double-sided polyptych commis-

sioned by Cardinal Stefaneschi for the high altar of the Basilica of St Peter sometime between 1300 and 1330. One of the panel works most widely thought to be by his own hand is the *Madonna in Majesty* once in All Saints, now in the Uffizi Gallery in Florence – an altarpiece "that is impressive and monumental with a sense of depth that seems difficult to collocate in Giotto's painting style earlier than the frescoes in Padua". The Master's presence in Florence is better documented from the second decade of the 14th century and the frescoes in the Peruzzi and Bardi Chapels situated in the right-side transept of the Franciscan Church of the Holy Cross are the last evidence of his fresco painting. The former depicts the *Lives of St John the Baptist and of St John the Evangelist*, while the latter continues the theme of his earlier works in Assisi, The *Life of St Francis*. Over the following centuries it was especially the frescoes in the

Peruzzi Chapel that were to enjoy particular fame, even Michelangelo copying some of the figures. Clearly that great patron of the arts, the Court of the Anjou at Naples, was to hear of Giotto's celebrity; and from December 1328 to some time in 1333 there is some evidence of his sojourn with Robert of Anjou: sadly, all works executed in that period have been lost. There is detailed evidence that on 12th April 1334 Giotto was nominated Master Builder of the Opera di Santa Reparata, now Santa Maria del Fiore, and the Commune's Superintendent of Public Works. According to Giovanni Villani's *Nuova Cronica*, that same year the foundation of the cathedral bell-tower was laid, based on plans by Giotto. The artist was able to follow the works down to the lower part of the plinth, until he died in 1337 while returning from Milan where the Florence Commune had sent him to lend his skills to Duke Azzone Visconti.

THE CHAPEL OF THE SCROVEGNI
HISTORY

A small, unadorned brick buil-ding whose architect has not been identified - some scholars have suggested Giovanni Degli Eremitani, others Giotto himself - the chapel was commissioned by Enrico Scrovegni. Perhaps it was in suffrage for the soul of his father, Reginaldo, who was made famous through those verses of Dante's in the XVII canto of the *Inferno* which accuse him of usury; and perhaps it was to forestall a similar destiny - espe-cially since he may have felt himself "tarred with the same brush". In point of fact, in the scene in the *Last Judgement* of the dedication of the chapel to the Blessed Virgin, Enrico appears dressed in violet, the colour of penitence, as he offers his sacred gift in symbolic restitution of what he had extracted by usury. Begun in 1303 and consecrated on 25 March 1305, the chapel was dedicated to Our Lady of the Annunciation. It was to serve as memorial chapel (Enrico Scrovegni, his wife, and two nephews are buried here) and private chapel, connected as it was to the palace that the Scrovegni had had built inside the Arena on land purchased from the Dalesmanini family in February 1300; this palace later became the property of the Foscari family and was demoli-shed in 1827.

The facade, in the hall-church style, is scanned in the upper parts by hanging arches and by a Gothic window of three mullions, and in the lower part by a door whose archivolt is of alternating white and reddish bricks; along the south wall is a row of six tall mullioned windows. The interior, featuring a barrel-vaulted nave, is subdivided by two small side altars. According to some scholars they were placed there during a later alteration, while others say that they were placed there as pulpits to separate the part reserved for the faithful from the Scrovegni family, who accessed their part through a small door at the end of the northern wall.

At the back, a polygonal apsidiole contains the *Sarcophagus of Enrico Scrovegni* (d.1336), attributed to Andriolo de' Santi; while on the altar are two Angel candle-bearers, and *The Virgin & Child* by Govanni Pisano.

It was Enrico Scrovegni who commissioned Giotto to execute the frescoes in the interior of the chapel, where the Master attained the height of his artistry, for this cycle of paintings signals "a point of no return in the entire history of western painting".

The work is attributed to the artist from Tuscany in a well-documented tradition, the first evidence dating back to the first decades of the 14th century. Scholars disagree as to the actual date of the decorations, although they unanimously accept 1305 as the date of the consecration of the edifice, since it is documented in a resolution passed by the Great Council in Venice on 16th March 1305 when approving a loan to Enrico Scrovegni, of some altar decorations from the Basilica of St Mark, for the consecration of a chapel of his proprietorship in Padua. It seems most likely, the-refore, that by this date the deco-rations in the chapel, if not com-plete, were well on the way to being so.

THE PAINTING CYCLE

On entering the Chapel, the observer is immediately attracted to the blue of the star-spangled vault of the ceiling, divided into two compartments by three bands, depicting the figures of the kings and the patriarchs of the Old Testament. In the central medallion, towards the entrance, is the *Virgin & Child*; in the part reserved for the Scrovegni family, *Christ the Saviour giving His Blessing*. From the outset, the importance of Mary's role is emphasised, for she will act as an intermediary on behalf of her Son for the gaining of Salvation – it is not by chance alone that the two complementary themes of the *Annunciation* (the beginning of the Christian salvation) and the *Last Judgement* (the end of the Christian experience) are placed facing each other. Her significant role is also shown by the unusual development of the scenes that tell of the lives of the Virgin's parents and of Mary herself who, furthermore, appears twice in the *Last Judgement* - as a guide to the elect, and then in the act of receiving the Chapel from its patron. The pictorial cycle follows a strict order and the scenes unfold in 38 panels covering three walls, on three levels, one above the other. It begins on the upper level of the right wall, near the arch of triumph, with the *Six Stories of Joachim*; continues, still on the upper level, along the opposite wall, starting from the entrance, with the *Six Stories of the Virgin*, as far as the two panels on the *Annunciation* on either side of the triumphal arch. The *Visitation*, underneath the figure of Our Lady of the Annunciation, completes the "early life" of Christ and the preamble to the Redemption.

The *Life of Jesus* begins on the middle level of the right wall, starting from the chancel arch and - spiralling as it unfolds - illustrates scenes from the Nativity to Pentecost. The individual panels are framed by ornamental bands with busts of the Saints and, in particular, in the second and third levels of the north wall, by scenes from the Old Testament. Along the lower level of the three walls there is an imitation marble plinth; in the nave this frames the monochromatic allegorical figures of the *Seven Virtues* (on the right) and the *Seven Vices* (on the left), facing each other. The natural conclusion to the message of Redemption is to be found on the interior face of the entrance wall, in *The Last Judgement*; on the left, on a level with the Vices, there is *Hell*, and on the right, as a continuation of the Virtues, is Paradise. Below *Christ the Judge* is the scene depicting Enrico Scrovegni in the act of presenting the chapel itself to Mary.

Recently the Chapel and its decorations have been the subject of various studies and even astronomical research in order to account for the extraordinary lighting effects that have been noticed in the interior - not withstanding the number of ancient trees outside impairing direct observation. It has been noticed that when the sun rises it shines through the first window towards the high altar, just to the left of the painting of the *Nativity*; and on Christmas Day, between 10 and 11, the ray of light shining through the window completely illuminates the little door through which the Scrovegni family members entered to attend the liturgical functions. At midday, this same bright ray illuminates the head of anyone standing on the axis of the chapel, in front of the steps of the high altar. Furthermore, after careful calculations, beginning with the calendar in use at the time of Giotto, it has been discovered that the part of the *Last Judgement* depicting the donation of the Chapel to the Madonna is lit up early in the morning by a slit of light that penetrates from a small hole placed above the first window immediately to the left of the entrance door, and that this occurs on the days of the most important Marian feast days (the Birth of Mary on the 8th September and on the Annunciation, 15th August).

Episodes from the lives of Joachim and Anne
1 Joachim is driven from the Temple
2 Joachim among the Shepherds
3 An Angel appears to St Anne
4 Joachim's Sacrifice
5 Joachim's Vision
6 Joachim and Anne's encounter

The Vices
a Foolishness
c Inconstancy
e Ire
g Injustice
i Idolatry
m Envy
o Despair

Episodes from the life of Mary
7 The Birth of Mary
8 Presentation in the Temple
9 The Consigning of the Branch Twigs
10 Prayer for the Budding of the Twigs
11 Mary & Joseph's Wedding
12 The Wedding Procession

Episodes from the life of Christ
13 God's command to the Archangel Gabriel respecting the Annunciation
14 The Visitation
15 The Birth of Jesus
16 The Adoration of the Wise Kings
17 The Presentation of Jesus in the Temple
18 The Flight into Egypt
19 The Slaughter of the Innocents
20 Jesus among the Scribes
21 The Baptism of Jesus
22 The Wedding in Cana
23 The Raising of Lazarus from the Dead
24 Jesus' Entrance into Jerusalem
25 The Merchants are driven from the Temple
26 Judas receives the Betrayal money

27 The Last Supper
28 The washing of the Feet
29 The Judas Kiss
30 Christ before Caiaphas
31 The Scourging of Christ
32 The climb to Calvary
33 The Crucifixion.
34 The Deposition
35 The Resurrection of Christ
36 The Ascension into Heaven
37 Pentecost

The Virtues
b Wisdom
d Fortitude
f Temperance
h Justice
l Faith
n Charity
p Hope

Drawing by Mariangela Baraldi

THE LIVES OF JOACHIM AND ANNE

RIGHT WALL:
UPPER LEVEL STARTING FROM THE CHANCEL ARCH
AND PROCEEDING TOWARDS THE ENTRANCE

1. Joachim is driven from the Temple
2. Joachim among the Shepherds
3. An Angel announces to Anne her Forthcoming Maternity
4. Joachim offers God a Sacrifice
5. Joachim's Vision
6. Joachim and Anne at the Aurea Gate

THE LIFE OF MARY

LEFT WALL:
UPPER LEVEL FROM THE ENTRANCE DOWN
TO THE CHANCEL ARCH

7. The Birth of Mary
8. Presentation of the Virgin in the Temple
9. The Consigning of the Branch Twigs
10. Prayer for the Budding of the Branch Twigs
11. The Wedding of Mary & Joseph
12. Mary returns to Nazareth

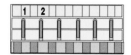
1. Joachim is driven from the Temple of Jerusalem

Joachim, having gone to the temple to offer a lamb in sacrifice, is driven out by the priest, Ruben, as he is deemed unworthy. By now an old man, he as yet has no offspring, signifying that he has not been blessed by God. The temple, shown aslant and diagonally across the corner of the picture, divides the scene into two parts. On the right, within the *sancta sanctorum*, where the Ark of the Covenant is kept, a scribe blesses one of the faithful; in the other part, the priest imperiously pushes Joachim out with his left hand and with his right tugs at his garment. Joachim's reaction is restrained and dignified; he holds his peace, clutching the animal to his heart, but his face shows his humiliation.
The features of the temple are kept to the essential, a pulpit, a canopy on fluted columns, a marble screen.

2. Joachim among the Shepherds

Joachim takes refuge in the mountains among the shepherds; he arrives with his head down, feeling quite miserable, not seeming even to notice the little dog that playfully welcomes him. Two shepherds deep in conversation have just come out of the sheep-cot with their flock and now exchange questioning glances. The figure of Joachim stands out clearly against the bare rocky background.
The naturalistic aspects are a new feature, especially as regards the animals.

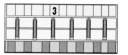

3. An Angel announces to Anne her Forthcoming Maternity

Silence sets the mood in this scene too, broken only by the unexpected apparition of the angel. Anne's house is a very simple setting, the same "spatial unit" that reappears further on in the *Birth of Mary*: the difference is in the psychological mood; here stillness reigns, there joyous confusion.

The divine event is placed in a familiar context: outside, under the portico, Judith the handmaiden is spinning; in the interior, the bed can be glimpsed through the white, partly drawn, curtain, a winding frame and bobbin are on the wall, and there is a shelf, and on the floor a chest.

4. Joachim offers God a Sacrifice

After the interval of the preceding scene, Joachim returns as protagonist. The priests have driven him away, the shepherds do not fully comprehend his suffering, but they stand by him. In the real desert of the mountain and the spiritual desert of the soul, Joachim seeks refuge in God to whom he sacrifices a goat on the altar, and God listens to him:

from on high He raises His hand in blessing and sends an angel to invite him to return to Jerusalem. The central scene of the sacrifice is framed by the figures of the shepherd and the angel; their almost specular hands guide our attention towards the Divine Hand: God listens to those who invoke His name.
Just above the altar, it is possible to make out a figure in prayer looking up to the sky.
The panel seems flawed by horizontal cracks.

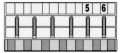

5. Joachim's Vision

Evening has come, the shepherds return to the sheep-cot. As Joachim falls into a deep sleep an angel appears to him and announces that his prayer has been granted.
The light emanating from the divine messenger lights up the surroundings and reflects off the shepherds garments. Giotto's narration proceeds contemporaneously: while in the meantime Joschim prays, Anne also prays, his wife already aware that she will become a mother.

6. Joachim and Anne at the Aurea Gate

A series of "group" scenes begin here, not interrupted until *The Annunciation*.
Joachim is about to arrive in Jerusalem with a shepherd; Anne goes to meet him, accompanied by a friend and by the handmaiden Judith, who holds a cloak over her left arm. On the bridge before the Aurea Gate the spouses finally meet up, "re-embrace" and kiss.
The flowing force of the "pyramid" that surrounds the spouses is notable. All present are joyful, only the widow friend almost completely wrapped in a black cloak does not join in the pleasure but gazes into a lost distance.
Some scholars have interpreted the gate as it is depicted, enclosed between two medieval towers and embattlements, as a reminder of the Arch of Augustus at Rimini, and claim the artist was present there before his arrival in Padua.

The story continues now on the west wall, from the entrance down. Notice the difference in the intensity of the light on the two walls: the south wall is illuminated by the three-light window of the facade, the west by the series of windows on the facing wall.

7. The Birth of Mary

We are in Anne's cottage, a joyous and vibrant scene because Mary has been born. Her friends and the handmaidens are all busy. One is presenting the swaddled baby to the mother, whose face lights up with joy as she reaches out to receive the daughter so long-desired. Two handmaidens have swathing bands draped over their shoulders, while another (it could be Judith) answers the door. In the foreground, yet another detail of everyday life: two handmaidens are looking after the baby. The older woman baths her, the younger one rolls up a cloth.

8. Presentation of the Virgin in the Temple

It is the day of Joachim's triumph; to that temple from which he was once so ignominiously cast out he now returns to present his daughter, Mary. The child is right in front of the high priest Abiatar; the splendour and the determination that emanates from such a small personage surprises the onlookers and the other older maidens, as well as the two priests, in the right foreground, who seem to be commenting on the scene. Behind Mary, her understandably proud parents are looking on, Anne lovingly pushing the child forward, more from maternal solicitude than any need to encourage her. Nearby, old Simeon observes the emotion on the face of Mary's father, Joachim.

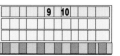

9. The Consigning of the Branch Twigs

The temple of Jerusalem is depicted in as many as four of the scenes along this wall. In the previous panel it is quite similar to that of *Joachim driven from the Temple*, though viewed from another angle; in this and in the following two panels, it is a little different and the "perspective" is frontal. Destiny has decreed that the one who is to be the protector of Mary, who has consecrated herself to God, is to be chosen from among the young celibates of the tribe of Judah. Each is to bring a branch to the temple and the one chosen from On High will see his put forth buds, or according to some scholars a dove should appear. The scene captures the moment in which Abiatar and the scribe Ruben receive the branch offerings and place them on the altar. The first figure on the left is Joseph, Mary's future spouse.

10. Prayer for the Budding of the Branch Twigs

This episode is not mentioned in the biblical texts on which Giotto based his work, except in the *Apocryphal Gospel of the Pseudo-Mathew*; for this reason many scholars maintain that the artist added the scene solely to balance the number of panels on facing walls. Mary's suitors and the high priest Abiatar pray intensely for the buds to appear on the branches. The youthful self-assurance of the preceding scene has changed to adoration. All are kneeling, staring at the altar, waiting for the divine portent. Who will be the chosen one? Joseph, no longer so young, stands to one side. The four figures in the foreground seem to be out in the open, which lends a deep perspective to the scene.

11. The Wedding of Mary & Joseph

Joseph is at the centre of the scene. God has chosen him, as is shown by the branch on which buds have appeared, and now he marries Mary of tender age as, dressed in white, she stands shyly before the company. It may be noted that Joseph has taken on the same face as Joachim, who will not appear any more; further on, this "facial type" will be seen to pass on to another figure.

The attitude of the "groups" is quite distinct: on one side three women and the scribe Ruben are concentrating on the ceremony, on the other side the youths seem more involved in showing their disappointment - even resentment - in not being chosen, by snapping the now useless branches.

This particular episode was to be echoed by Raphael in his *Marriage of the Virgin* in Brera.

12. Mary returns to Nazareth

Mary advances with elegant gait towards her father's house, of which we can discern the loggia with two mullioned windows decorated with trefoils, typical of French Gothic. Following her are seven nubile handmaidens, recognisable from their long flowing hair.

According to some scholars the scene represents Mary's return to her parents in Nazareth, accompanied by the handmaidens and three musicians; others believe that it is the wedding procession - but how to explain Joseph's absence?
Interpretation is rendered even more difficult by the panel's poor state of conservation.

13. The Archangel's Mission to Mary

This most unusual subject occupies the whole lunette of the wall of the triumphal arch. Amidst a host of angels, God the Father engages the Archangel Gabriel to announce to Mary that she will conceive a son. The Almighty is depicted seated on His throne, of which there is a perspective of three steps. The scene is on a wooden panel set into a niche: probably there was originally a window here that was later closed over to avoid breaking the continuity of the narration. The solemn, Byzantine-like image shows God as unusually young with brown beard and hair; he is speaking with a fixed look, and with a gesture of his right hand. The host of angels form a circle around him; some seem to have bodies, some appear as though suspended in the sky, others sing or sound instruments.

The Annunciation

Inevitably, upon entering, the visitor glances towards the triumphal arch that stands opposite, and the first scene that comes into focus is *The Annunciation*; and looking up, there is the blue starry sky with the star of the *Virgin*, mother and queen in the centre. So the significance of the Madonna to this chapel is immediately apparent. The gestures held in the scene are "theatrical" and posed in the manner of sacred works. Separated by the respective pillars of the arch, the two protagonists are nonetheless joined by the twin architectural features of the house of Nazareth which almost mirror each other. Under the two small balconies, from one of which white drapes hang, there is a real *trait d'union* between the two parts, in the form of a traditional frontal perspective that provides the spatial "unit" where the announcement takes place. The figure of Gabriel the Archangel is bathed in light (notice the shades of rose colour) shining full on the face of Mary, transfiguring it. The chiaroscuro of her garment defines the volume of her body that now shows up majestically - no longer that of a young girl, but of a woman.

14. The Visitation

This panel opens the story of the infancy and public life of Christ, that takes place on the second level, and dramatically concludes with Judas' betrayal, on the opposite pillar of the arch. Maria, accompanied by two handmaidens has come to visit her cousin Elizabeth who has been pregnant for some months. The two women greet each other and embrace; both have a child in the womb, both are mothers by Divine Will.

Mary's garment and the arrangement of her hair are already different from in the preceding panel: she wears a richly ornamented red gown and her hair is gathered in a bun, sign of her being a married woman. Notice, in fact, how Giotto has muted the colours of the clothes of the main characters according to their age and situation.

15. The Birth of Jesus

Propped against a rock cavity is the hut where Mary and Joseph have taken refuge and where Jesus was born. As a pictorial statement it is hardly new, it so clearly recalls the Byzantine tradition and the pulpits of Nicola and Giovanni Pisano. Giotto's originality lies in the naturalness of the gestures, the looks and reactions -

the way the Virgin stretches out as she raises herself to take her son from a woman who is passing him towards her; and Joseph's falling asleep with the flock is realistic, where only one sheep is awake licking her lamb.

In relation to the Baby, all the figures in the composition are placed in a circular arrangement with a movement that seems to proceed from left towards right. The angels themselves seem orientated in the same direction as the movement of the sun that enters in the morning through the window placed on the left side of the fresco and sets in the evening on the right side of anyone observing the scene.

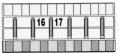

16. The Adoration of the Wise Kings

The Wise Kings guided by the comet have come to Bethlehem to honour the Child Jesus with precious gifts. The kneeling Melchior has taken off his crown and offers gold (the vase that the angel holds in his hand), Balthazar the myrrh oil (in the horn of plenty), Gaspar, the youngest, the incense. The densely "packed" scenic style is within the tradition; but here, by using the two camels the artist has borrowed a novelty from Giovanni Pisano; and he has inserted a genial and lively glimpse of the face of the camel driver, viewed from below, as he looks up at the capricious beast. The representation of the comet is curious too, as, according to many scholars, it could be Halley's Comet, that had appeared in the sky a few years before the chapel was decorated.

17. The Presentation of Jesus in the Temple

At the centre, supported by fluted pillars, is the same canopy as in *Joachim driven from the Temple*; since that day of humiliation at least two generations have passed! Now very advanced in years, Simeon (112), has received little Jesus in his arms, who however looks startled, kicks, and puts his hand out for his mother. Mary instinctively reaches for her little son to take him to her breast. This spontaneous central narrative is framed, on the right, by an angel and the elderly prophetess Anna and, on the left, by an elegantly dressed female figure and Joseph - who has brought two doves as gifts.

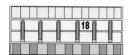

18. The Flight into Egypt

The real centre of the scene is the triangle enclosing the group consisting of Mary, Jesus and the donkey - in its turn set against the rocky pyramid of the mountainside.

Joseph flees towards Egypt having been warned by an angel that King Herod has ordered all infants under two years to be slaughtered. The fugitives are accompanied by four youths, three behind and one ahead, and the angel of the Lord who is showing the way.

The characters are silent: the Virgin is deep in thought and holds the Baby tightly between her arms, whilst Joseph half turns to glances almost furtively at his beloved ones.

In these last four panels the original colour effect has been partly reduced and altered by the disappearance of the azurite from the garments of some of the characters, particularly from the Madonna's cloak.

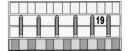

19. The Slaughter of the Innocents

One of the most dramatic scenes in the cycle is when King Herod orders the slaughter of the infants with the intention of killing Jesus.
The scene pivots around the hired ruffian who is about to impale an infant; our gaze follows the child's struggles as he clutches desperately to his mother, then shifts to the single mob of wailing, weeping women. This group then seems to form a solid block which continues into the octagonal edifice that stands in the background.
Our gaze now spirals to the building on the left where stands the ignoble king, it proceeds towards the lower foreground and comes to rest on the heap of slaughtered infants - "lifeless white stones".
Even the three soldiers on the left are upset, one of them cannot bear the sight of such atrocity.

20. Jesus among the Scribes

In the interior of the temple of Jerusalem, Jesus - who has just turned twelve - discourses with the Doctors of the Law. Standing on the left are Mary and Joseph who have been anxiously searching for Him. This gospel scene is set in an ample spatial dimension. The perspective of the ten elders is arranged so as to suggest the vastness of the central hall with its large apse which frames the Divine Child, and arches leading through to the aisles.
The figures of the learned scribes have a certain stiffness, but what stands out is the sudden movement of the head of the third one from the left as he turns at the arrival of the parents of Jesus. The fresco's very poor condition is due to the saline condition of the wall.

21. The Baptism of Jesus

Jesus, by now an adult, lets himself be baptised by John the Baptist. The Trinity is at the centre of the scene: high in the opening of the sky there is the Eternal Father and, below him (the deterioration makes it almost indiscernible) the dove of the Holy Spirit, as they bless the Son of God, who stands immersed in the clear waters of the Jordan. A white, supernatural light illuminates Christ's pale skin, the angel, the mountain, and the Baptist's rose-coloured mantle. This is the moment Jesus begins his public life, and his double nature, both human and divine, is symbolically emphasised by the colour of his clothes, the red of the tunic and the blue of his cloak (the latter, sadly, almost completely lost).

22. The Wedding in Cana

Jesus and Mary have been invited to a wedding feast in the city of Cana.
As there is no wine left, Jesus changes the water into wine. Giotto captures the moment when the divine blessing causes the miracle to happen and the Master of Ceremony personally verifies the miraculous event. The strong characterisation of

this stout personage would suggest that it is a real-life portrait. As in *Jesus among the Scribes*, the scene gives a sense of space, even though it shows an interior. The horizontal and diagonal lines of the balcony and quatrefoil wall decorations are echoed in the table layout, lending width and depth to the composition, while the vertical lines of the wall-hangings give an impression of height.

23. The Raising of Lazarus from the Dead

Another "external" rock scene, here the tomb of Lazarus, Jesus' friend, has been excavated and Jesus grants Martha (sister of the dead man) and Mary their wish: to the general astonishment of the curious onlookers he brings back to life a body that has lain dead for some days. Notice, in fact, the two figures to the right of the still-bandaged corpse who cover their faces to protect themselves from the nauseous stench.
Particularly vivacious is the figure of the young man in the centre with his right hand raised. On the left, outlined against the deep blue sky, a priest-like Christ is giving his blessing.

24. Jesus' Entrance into Jerusalem

On one side the apostles are following Christ who is mounted on a lowly donkey; on the other side there is the rejoicing crowd of citizens from Jerusalem who have come out of the city to encounter him.
In the background, two boys are climbing up the olive trees and snapping off branches to wave in honour of Jesus; in the foreground, a young man has spread his cloak before the animal's hoofs - the one at the back of him is trying to get his cloak off but his head is stuck in it; a third is pulling at a sleeve of his own coat in an effort to take it off.
The apostles, especially Peter and Andrew, seem surprised at such a commotion.

25. Jesus Drives the Merchants from the Temple

The gentle Christ giving his benediction, that was noted in the three preceding panels, has now changed to fury: the House of God has been transformed into "a den of thieves" by the merchants and money-changers and the god that they adore is money.
Jesus reacts by upsetting the tables and benches and anything in his way: the animals flee, a cage is empty, the hand that blessed now takes up a cord and whips a young man.
Two little boys take refuge among the apostles; Peter hides one under his cloak.
Further back on the right, two high priests do not seem to approve of Jesus' behaviour. The import of the scene is unequivocally rendered by the dominating presence of the temple, in a slightly "foreshortened" perspective, the central arch of the portico framing the figure of Christ. Many scholars have remarked on the statues of the two horses and two lions above the portico as an evident allusion to Venice.

26. Judas' Betrayal

The prologue to the Passion, Death and Resurrection.
Judas Iscariot, driven by the devil, makes a pact with the high priests Caiaphas and Anna to consign Jesus to them. The characterisation of Judas is here quite pronounced both in the hawk-nosed Jewish profile and in the yellow of his cloak - the colour of betrayal.
But it is the hands that speak most strongly in this scene: those of the devil and of Anna reassuring Judas, the left hand of the apostle that holds on tightly to the purse containing the 30 pieces of silver, and Caiaphas' unmistakable gesture as he points out the traitor to an official of the temple.

27. The Last Supper

Before he is to die, Jesus brings all his disciples together for a feast. During the meal he remarks, "One of you will betray me". Giotto captures the apostles' reactions: each one wonders about himself and questions his neighbour. Peter, on Jesus' left, seems to have stiffened; John rests his head on the Masters breast; Judas - his back to us - dressed in yellow, reaches out to take the piece of bread that Jesus has just dipped into the bowl.

The gospel story is faithfully drawn and set in a strictly geometrical perspective: a portico delimited by two bare walls (once decorated) and two slender pillars in the foreground. Originally the haloes were all gold, but Jesus' made of true fine gold has endured, whilst the others have been blackened by chemical reactions. It may be noted that Judas has a halo devoid of rays.

28. Jesus Washes the Feet of the Apostles

This scene is strictly related to the preceding one both in its setting and atmosphere. Jesus having hitched up his garment with a strip of cloth begins to wash the apostles' feet. He kneels before Peter who raises his vest to offer his right leg. John is standing, holding the bowl of water. Glancing up, one cannot help but be struck by the parallel between this panel and the two above: *Anne* (Mary's mother) *in Prayer*, the higher of the two, and The *Adoration of the Wise Men*. In all three the central figure is kneeling, although the significance varies. Notice too how the same face formerly represen-

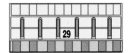

ting Joachim's and then Joseph's has now become St Peter's.

29. The Kiss of Betrayal

Due to its tense dramatic impact this is justifiably one of the most famous scenes. In the garden of Gethsemane where Jesus and the apostles have retired to pray, Judas arrives guiding the soldiers; he embraces and kisses the Master so that the victim can be identified. The priest Caiaphas follows him and indicates Jesus with his right hand. Around the sculpted block of Judas' yellow cloak that completely covers Christ - around those two profiles that touch and look so intensely at each other - there is a whirling of lances, pikes, torches and staves; there are shouts and trumpet blasts, there is Peter's violent reaction as he cuts a soldier's ear while, viewed from the rear, a hooded figure tugs his cloak. From the three closely aligned groups in the foreground the focus shifts to certain well-drawn countenances in the middle ground, and straight afterwards to the uniform mass of soldiers' helmets. This crush of bodies further distinguishes the main protagonists of the scene illuminated in the torchlight, flames in the dark of the night revealing the tragedy.

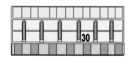

30. Christ before Anna and Caiaphas

The perspective in this and the successive panel are identical, only the scene of the action changes. Jesus is now alone in the hands of his enemies; he is brought before the high priest Anna and the latter's son-in-law Caiaphas who begin to interrogate him. His reply causes a strong response among those present: Caiaphas rends his own garment, two common soldiers protest, one turning towards Anna, the other to the soldier who is about to cuff Christ, as though approving the gesture.

This explosion of violent passion contrasts with the disarming meekness of Jesus who turns as though in a daze to look at the soldier.

31. The Scourging of Christ

From Anna the priest's house Jesus has been taken to that of the Roman governor Pontius Pilate for judgement. In Giotto's picture the "judgement" has already been passed and Pilate is washing his hands; to please the priests he delivers the innocent into the hands of the soldiers seeming, in fact, to say: "There, see what an end he has

come to, isn't that enough for you?" The hub of the action revolves around Jesus. After having draped a regal mantle about him, seven fellows mal-treat him - notice the portrayal of their grim features - pull his beard, mock him, and kneel before him addressing him as "King of the Jews". Giotto's interpretation of the gospel chapter is certainly original con-sidering the scarce importance he attributes to Pilate; but espe-cially new, one could almost say *modern*, is his refined use of colour - as in the particularly striking figure of the black man dressed in white, at the centre of the scene.

32. Jesus climbs to Calvary

The gate of Jerusalem, the scene a few days earlier of Christ's triumphal entry to shouts of jubilation from the citizens, where now a man curved under the weight of a cross passes through, goaded on like an ani-mal, guarded like a common felon by soldiers. The proces-sion moves along slowly, led by two youths one of whom, barefooted, turns as though to point out the way. Jesus, agoni-sed and humiliated, turns towards a fellow who is vilely beating him with a stick on the shoulders, and his face bears that same mild and perplexed expression as in the panel *Christ before Caiaphas and Anna*.
On the left side, Mary tries to follow her son to the place of execution but is roughly turned away by a soldier. Although the state of conservation leaves much to be desired, one may note the spatial depth around the figures in the procession, which Giotto achieved by refi-ned touches.

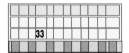

33. The Crucifixion

For the subject most commonly depicted in the Christian world, Giotto has created a composition largely following traditional lines. Well may the anguish of the angels around the cross already have been a feature of Cimabue's *Crucifixion* at Assisi, but the innovation here is the spiralling movement, obtained by an adept foreshortening of the figures. The naturalness and intensity of the gestures and expressions is especially original. On the left, a very wan-looking Mary, mother of Jesus, is held up by Mary of Cleophas and John the Apostle. At the centre, the Crucified one who is dead - occupying the full height of the panel; Mary Magdalen kneeling at his feet, drying his blood with her hair. On the right, the soldiers share out Jesus' clothes but are unsure whether to cut the red tunic "in one piece woven". The chromatic effect on the mantle that has fallen at Mary Magdalen's feet is very delicate, and the transparency of Christ's loin-cloth is another very precious effect. In this scene it is clearer than ever that it was Giotto's intention to render the emotions of the figures, particularly poignant in the expression of suffering on the faces of the Madonna and Mary Magdalen and in the weeping angels.

34. Weeping over the Body of Christ

Here Giotto is at the height of his artistry.
Every line, look and gesture leads to the two faces - the mother's and her dead son's. Mary's desperation is written in her eyes which are shadowed with grief.
Starting from this, our attention shifts by and by to the anguish of the menfolk, of nature itself, and of the angels. Humanity is represented by the pious women, by John with arms outspread, by the inconsolable Mary Magdalen, by Nicodemus and Joseph of Arimathea.
The dramatic event has marked Nature itself which is bare and deserted, the single tree - dry, almost skeletal.
The flowing lines of the two sculpturesque figures in the foreground make a strong impression; they have their backs to us and seem to be almost emerging from the panel itself.
Clearly evident are the lessons learned from the classical models studied during his trips to Rome.
The personages acquire stature through the chiaroscuro effect and the encircling lines, assuming the monumentality of ancient statuary.

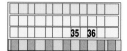

35. The Resurrection

In the left foreground, five soldiers are fast asleep next to the by now empty sepulchre on which two angels are seated. On the right, Mary Magdalen is kneeling and reaching towards the risen Christ who stops her with a gesture of his hand. The subject is also known as *Noli me tangere* (Thou must not touch me). Light pervades the whole picture, shining on the front of the images, the rose marble, the white vexillum proclaiming the words *Victor mortis* (the victor of death), and onto the mountain slope. The chromatic effect is further accentuated by the contrast between the candid garment of Jesus and the red of Mary Magdalen's cloak. Oddly enough, the two tree trunks in the background have no foliage - the result of some clumsy retouching of the paint. In the foreground on the right, the trampled bushes, grass and leaves are precious clues to Christ's having risen.

36. The Ascension

The Resurrected Christ - in the golden mandorla - ascends into the sky, his hands already disappearing out of the picture frame. He is at the centre of an imaginary cross sustained at the base by two completely delineated angels who are pointing with their hands to Jesus, while the cross-arms consist of hosts of angels and saints on either side. Each figure seems weightless, drifting upwards, drawn by the Risen Christ, a sensation intensified by the solid figures of the apostles and of the Madonna as they watch the event. Many onlookers are holding up their hands to protect themselves

from the dazzling gaze of the Son of God. The apostle in the right foreground is notable for the refined elegance and embroidery of his white mantle.

37. Pentecost

The architectural setting is clearly outlined: through six gothic windows we perceive the Apostles gathered together to receive the Holy Spirit. The gift which will enable them to explain themselves and communicate with all people is descending in the form of rays of light that strike the heads of the twelve. Their facial expressions and the colours of the Apostles' garments are always consistent and inevitably are compared to those in *The Last Supper*, situated on the opposite wall. Besides their identical perspective - although in this panel the apostles are arranged in another mode – the differences between the two scenes lies more in the type of light: on the south wall it is nightfall; here it is almost clear daylight, and brightened further by the natural light that enters from the window on the opposite side. It is also interesting to note how Peter, the apostle in the second row on the left, turns to gaze at the spectator, almost as though to show which course to take next. Peter, the successor to Christ, the representative of the Church, is the mediator between the models of the Christian life (Mary and Jesus) and the temporal conditions of man (the virtues and vices).

WALL OF THE CENTRAL CHANCEL ARCH

The two "tromp l'oeil" chambers

Painted on either side of the triumphal arch, in correspondence to the third level, there are two *trompe l'oeil* views that are without iconographic precedence. Scholars consider them as the point of departure for pictorial perspective in the modern sense. The two cross-vaulted chapels featuring gothic two-light mullioned windows are shown in perspective but on a diverging plane from the small balconies of the *Annunciation* (on the same wall). Behind two fictive marble buttresses two chambers are perceived, and hanging from their ceilings, at the cross-point of the two vaulting ribs, are two metallic cylinder-shaped lanterns each with nine lamps; and there are large panel sections on the walls - as though ready to be frescoed.
By standing in the centre of the chapel it is possible to appreciate the effects of light and colour and to acquire a view of the perspective in relation to the axis of the apse.
Here Giotto shows his perfect mastery of the laws of perception which he applies in these pictorial and architectural decorations. According to recent scholarship, these two examples of "trompe l'oeil" might show the transept as it was intended to be, but never carried out.
It is true that by examining the *Last Judgement* painted above the interior wall of the entrance, and by observing the little scale model of the chapel that Enrico Scrovegni is offering to the Madonna and to two saints, it is possible to perceive a transept, or in any case a system of chapels in the vicinity of the apse. According to some scholars, these chapels were to shelter the tombs of Enrico and Reginaldo Scrovegni.

ORNAMENTAL MOTIFS OF THE WALLS

All the wall panels are framed by decorative elements; on the first level the alternation is regular, as in the second and third levels of the left wall; instead, on the right wall the dividers are windows. Within each row there are one, two, or three multifoiled squares with busts of the prophets, saints and doctors of the Church. They adhere to a devotional programme strictly connected to the essential message of the whole cycle of frescoes – man's progress towards redemption.
The five central vertical dividers of the left wall - corresponding to the windows in the facing wall - merit particular attention.
Episodes from the Old Testament are depicted in the centre of the second and third levels within quatrefoil panels; these prefigure the scenes from the life and passion of Jesus.
These juxtapositions and parallels which medieval biblical exegesis was quite fond of are in some cases evident and self-explanatory, while in others they are harder to interpret.

- *Circumcision – Baptism*
- *Moses causes water to flow from the rock – The Miracle of Cana (water turned into wine)*
- *The Creation of Man – The Lazzarus is brought back to life*
- *The sons of the prophets of Jericho going to encounter the prophet Elisha – Jesus' entrance into Jerusalem*
- *Michael the Archangel defeats the dragon – The merchants are driven from the Temple*
- *Moses has the brass serpent raised to save the people of Israel – The Crucifixion of Christ*
- *Jonah three days in the belly of the whale – Christ three days in the tomb*
- *A young lion warms her cubs with her breath – Resurrection*
- *Elijah carried off in the sky above a chariot of fire – the Ascension*
- *Ezekiel devours a book and tells the people of Israel of its contents – The Holy Spirit descends*

VAULT

The work on the vault is separated into two sections by three transverse bands. Above the *Last Judgement*, the first band depicts the prophets of the Old Testament, as does the central band; the third, above the triumphal arch, pictures the ten patriarchs. Hundreds of eight-sided stars twinkle all over the vault. In the first section, five tondi with gold backgrounds show off the glowing images of Our Lady of Charity and the four prophets (*Malachi, Daniel, Isaiah, and Baruch*) who foretold of Mary's maternity. In the second section, the *Redeemer* is placed in the centre and arranged around it are the prophets *Ezekiel, Jeremiah* and *Micah* who foretold of the birth of the Messiah, and there is also the *Baptist*.

FOURTH OR LOWEST LEVEL

THE ALLEGORIES OF THE VIRTUES & VICES

The fourth row is placed almost at eye-level above a fictive marble plinth, and depicts the allegories of the virtues on the right and the vices on the left.

After meditating on the lives of Mary and Jesus, the faithful are now brought face to face with reality, the choice between Good and Evil - and the message is made quite clear.

For, from the panel of the Pentecost, the cycle proceeds from the interior towards the entrance wall and the Last Judgement, which for Christians represents the conclusive moment of human destiny.

It is by observing the picture of the day of Divine Judgement that we see how Evil ways lead directly to the damned in Hell; it is not by chance that the series of Vices culminates in Despair. Instead, on the opposite wall, Hope flies towards the Paradise of the blessed: by choosing the Virtues the Good are guided to salvation.

The representations of the Virtues and Vices are in monochrome and are arranged inside fictive marble niches, each identifiable by a name "engraved" on the architrave, by a series of symbols that give each a special character, and by the inscription on the base, which however is not always completely legible.

The best way to grasp the significance of these allegories is to proceed from that immediately under the Pentecost, that is, *Pride*, and from there to shift to the contrasting virtue, *Prudence*, and so on, as follows:

Foolishness – Wisdom; Inconstancy – Fortitude; Ire – Temperance; Injustice – Justice; Infidelity, Idolatry – Faith; Envy – Charity; Despair – Hope.

a Foolishness
This is an oddly adorned masculine figure, with his mouth closed by a lock, and holding a cudgel in his right hand. The head covered in feathers and the long tail, similar to a peacock's, symbolise fickleness and fatuity.

b Wisdom
A feminine figure seated at a writing desk looks at herself in the mirror and, turning round, reveals behind her head the presence of a bearded masculine profile. She not only looks back to the past and thus learns from experience, but also takes lessons from the book in front of her.

c Inconstancy
A young woman tries in vain to balance on a wheel that descends a slope: a life based on whims instead of firm principles can only slide further downhill.

d Fortitude
This is a powerful image of a woman holding a shield and clutching an iron club in her right hand. She wears a lion's head and her bust is protected by armour; fortitude is a crusader.

e Ire

Here is one of the most powerful of all the images in the allegories; the violent gesture of the hands ripping the garment, baring the breast, recall a similarly angry reaction by Caiaphas before Jesus in panel no.19.

f Temperance

Such violence is met by meekness and clemency. The woman is indeed grasping a sword, but she has rendered it inoffensive by tying it with knots and bands. Even the tongue should be controlled: to "guide" the words a bridle must be put over the mouth.

g Injustice

This quite complex figure is placed in the centre of the wall: there is the large figure of an old man framed in the arch of the gateway of a ruined castle; he is holding a sword and a grappling-iron in his hands; before him grow the trees of evil which are evident in the brutality and violence of the images of the frieze.

h Justice

"Perfect justice weighs everything with great equity…" begins the inscription beneath the frieze, and there is a feminine figure seated on a large gothic throne who holds in her hands the scales of justice bearing two angels: the one on the right side of Justice is crowning a wise man (unfortunately, the image has almost completely disappeared), while the other is smiting a wicked man with his sword. The effects of a just and good government are represented in the frieze beneath with scenes of hunting, dancing and riding.

i Unfaithfulness

As this allegory is to be interpreted in a religious key, it is also called Idolatry or Paganism. Turning his back on God, who appears at the top right, the infidel holds an idol in his hand, that in turn holds him tied to his collar by a cord. His destiny is the fires of Hell.

l Faith

This is a solemn and stately image. The feminine figure holds a cross in her right hand and in the left a scroll symbolising revealed truth; with the staff of the cross she is destroying an idol and knocking down two tablets bearing symbols of the cabbala.

m Envy

The envious one is the first victim of his own vice, and the serpent issuing from the mouth of this female figure rebels against her. The fires of Hell and the burning desire for things belonging to others devour her.

n Charity

This young woman, wreathed in flowers, reaching out her hand towards God who offers her a bag - the symbol of providence - is considered one of the paintings with the highest stylistic quality among the Virtues and Vices. The basket laden with pomegranates, which she is holding in her right hand, is particularly beautiful.

o Despair

Here is the most tragic picture in the allegoric cycle: the hanged man dangles dramatically, his limbs stiff, while the demon grabs him by the hair with a hook. At the Last Judgement – Hell awaits him.

p Hope

The young winged maiden, trusting in God, flies up towards an angel who crowns her and guides her into Paradise.

THE LAST JUDGEMENT

This fresco occupies the whole area of the interior wall above the main entrance. The iconographic plan is traditional. At the centre, under the three-light window, there is Christ the Father, in a glowing oval inset, who with a gesture separates the good from the wicked. The separation is further emphasised by a high cross held by two angels, to the left of which two choirs advance, guided by the angels. That of the saints, nearer to God the Father, includes the Blessed Virgin and the Blessed of the Old Testament and of the early Church; the Choir of the Elect – lower down – represents the people of God in all their diversity: men and women, religious or lay people, rich and poor, kings and queens, soldiers and farmers, etc. According to tradition, the fourth personage from the left among the Elect, with a white hat on his head, is Giotto himself. Just above the frame of the fresco, the dead are coming out of the bare rock of the tomb - it is the resurrection of the flesh, and it is exactly at this point that the artist has inserted a devotional reminder: Enrico Scrovegni who, kneeling, offers the small model of the Chapel, to the Blessed Virgin who is in the centre, and to Saints Catherine and John the Evangelist at the side. Some experts maintain that the friar who is holding the chapel could be the one who devised the theological plans on which the entire decorative cycle is based. On the left of the central cross is the pit of Hell. Four tongues of fire leap from the oval panel, separating the damned

and causing them to fall towards Lucifer - tormented and dragged down by the demons. The serenity, the dignity and order of the host of angels and the Blessed are in complete contrast to their desperation, frenzied agitation and chaos.

Among the damned are many usurers who can be identified by the white sack they have around the neck; on the extreme right Judas can be glimpsed, who has been hanged with others on a branch.

At the side of Christ in Judgement are the twelve Apostles seated on thrones placed on a semicircular dais. Higher up is a host of angels. In the highest point two angels are rolling aside the blue vault with the sun and the moon, and the "new skies and new land" are revealed.

THE PRESBYTERY AND APSE

The pictorial decoration is not the work of Giotto but of an unknown follower known as the "Master of the Scrovegni Choir". The cycle was executed towards the end of the second decade of the 14th century and represents the last episodes of the life of the Madonna.

Left wall, from top to bottom: *The foretelling of the Death of Mary, The Apostles say Goodbye to Mary, The Death of Mary.*

Right wall, from bottom to top: *The Funeral of the Blessed Virgin, The Assumption of Mary into Heaven, The Coronation of Mary.*

THE STATUES BY GIOVANNI PISANO

The altar dedicated to the Virgin Mary is to be found in the apse, and above it are three marble statues, the work of Giovanni Pisano, commissioned by Enrico Scrovegni probably on the advice of Giotto himself.

The side statues represent two *Candle-bearing Angels*, the central one the *Madonna and Child*.

The artist has signed his work with the following inscription along the base of the central statue: DEO GRATIAS – IO H(AN)IS MAGISTRI NICOLI – DE PISIS, but the other two are also initialled.

According to most experts, the three statues would have been realised by 1305, the year the Chapel was consecrated.

The artistic level is high indeed, especially the *Madonna*.

In her figure, in the elegant spreading of the pleats of her gown, in the modulated bending of her body, the expression of her face that turns to gaze anxiously at the Infant that smiles at her and struggles towards her, we feel the same intense humanity experienced in the pictures of Giotto himself.

THE SEPULCHRE OF ENRICO SCROVEGNI

The sarcophagus of Enrico Scrovegni lies behind the high altar. He died in Venice on 30th August 1336 and was buried in his Chapel in Padua on 23rd November of the same year. The tombstone shows Scrovegni lying on the sepulchre. Scholars have not yet agreed to whom to attribute the work although the most likely candidate is Andriolo de' Santi.

THE CRUCIFIXION

This panel is conserved in the Civic Museum.
It has a gilded, raised, mixed linear external profile.
On the main face, there is the *Christ Crucifix*, depicted on a very precious background similar to an oriental textile, *Our Lady of Sorrows* and *St John the Evangelist* on the sides, while on high there is the image of the

Redeemer.
On the other side is *The Mystic Lamb* and the symbol of the four evangelists.
The work was not therefore originally mounted on a wall, but may have been attached to the iconostasis or collocated halfway along the nave, where the two altars dedicated to Saints Catherine and John the Evangelist are found.

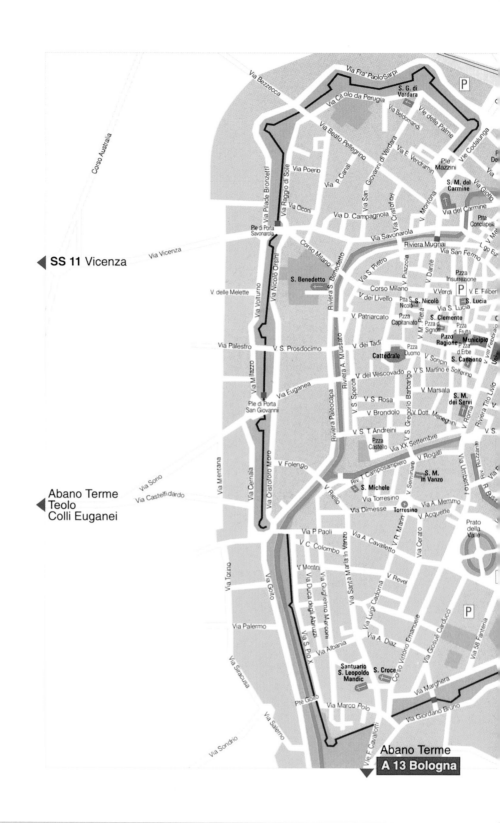